Get Smarter

SUPER FUN

Travel

ACTIVITIES

to Baffle
Your Brain

Brimming with creative inspiration, how-to projects, and useful information to enrich your everyday life, Quarto Knows is a favorite destination for those pursuing their interests and passions. Visit our site and dig deeper with our books into your area of interest: Quarto Creates, Quarto Cooks, Quarto Homes, Quarto Lives, Quarto Drives, Quarto Explores, Quarto Gifts, or Quarto Kids.

© 2018 Quarto Publishing Group USA Inc.

First Published in 2018 by MoonDance Press, an imprint of The Quarto Group. 6 Orchard Road, Suite 100, Lake Forest, CA 92630, USA. T (949) 380-7510 F (949) 380-7575 **www.QuartoKnows.com**

MoonDance Press titles are also available at discount for retail, wholesale, promotional, and bulk purchase. For details, contact the Special Sales Manager by email at specialsales@quarto.com or by mail at The Quarto Group, Attn: Special Sales Manager, 401 Second Avenue North, Suite 310, Minneapolis, MN 55401 USA.

ISBN: 978-1-63322-550-3
Digital edition published in 2018
eISBN: 978-1-63322-551-0

Written by Joe Rhatigan
Cover design and layout by Melissa Gerber

Printed in China
10 9 8 7 6 5 4 3 2 1

Get SMaRTeR

SUPER FUN
Travel
ACTIVITIES

to Baffle YOUR Brain

MoonDance

ARE WE THERE YET?

IT'S VACATION TIME, AND WHETHER YOU'RE IN A CAR, ON A PLANE, IN A BOAT, OR ON A TRAIN, SOONER OR LATER YOU WILL HAVE THE URGE TO UTTER, "ARE WE THERE YET?" THE ANSWER IS "NO." YOU KNOW THAT'S THE ANSWER, BUT YOU ASK ANY WAY. WHY? BECAUSE YOU'RE BORED OUT OF YOUR MIND. WELL, NOW YOU HAVE SOMETHING FUN AND TIME-CONSUMING TO DO *WITH* YOUR MIND BEFORE YOU LOSE IT: THIS AWESOME BOOK FILLED WITH THINGS TO DO, GAMES TO PLAY, CHALLENGES TO ACCOMPLISH, AND PUZZLES TO SOLVE. GRAB A PENCIL AND START WITH THE EASY STUFF AT THE BEGINNING OR DIVE RIGHT INTO THE CHALLENGING STUFF TOWARD THE BACK OF THE BOOK. DO THE ACTIVITIES BY YOURSELF OR INVITE YOUR TRAVELING COMPANIONS TO GET INVOLVED. YOU'LL HAVE SO MUCH FUN THAT YOU WON'T CARE THAT YOU'RE NOT THERE YET.

ON THE ROAD SCAVENGER HUNT

WHILE DRIVING TOWARD YOUR VACATION DESTINATION, GET EVERYONE INVOLVED IN LOOKING FOR THE FOLLOWING ITEMS. CIRCLE THE ONES YOU FIND.

1. CAR WITH FLAT TIRE

2. BIRDS ON A WIRE

3. TRUCK CARRYING ANIMALS

4. A CHURCH

5. BLANK BILLBOARD

6. DOG IN A CAR WINDOW

7. PERSON WITH FEET ON DASHBOARD

8. KID IN A CHILD SEAT

9. CAR WITH STICKERS ON WINDOW

10. CAR WITH AT LEAST 7 BUMPER STICKERS

11. LICENSE PLATE FROM ANOTHER COUNTRY

12. ANIMAL ON SIDE OF THE ROAD

13. YIELD SIGN

14. PERSON IN CAR SINGING

15. CAR WITH AT LEAST THREE BIKES ON IT

16. PICKUP TRUCK PULLING A CAMPER

17. TRACTOR TRAILER WITH A PICTURE OF A PERSON ON IT

18. PIECES OF A TIRE ON THE ROAD

19. HITCHHIKER

20. COW

YOUR AD HERE!

DESIGN YOUR OWN BILLBOARDS!

MINI CROSSWORDS

EASY PEASY: USE THE CLUES TO HELP YOU FILL IN THE BLANKS.
ANSWERS ON PAGE 91.

THE NOISES ANIMALS MAKE

ACROSS

1. CAT
3. HORSE
5. DOG
7. DUCK

DOWN

2. PIG
4. SNAKE
6. LION

BUGS THAT BOTHER

ACROSS

3. OPPOSITE OF "TOCKS"
5. THEY BUZZ IN YOUR EAR
6. YELLOW JACKETS OR HORNETS

DOWN

1. THEY RUIN PICNICS
2. THEY DRAW BLOOD
4. THEY HAVE A HIVE MENTALITY
5. THEY LIVE ON YOUR PETS

GETTING AROUND

ACROSS

1. ON THE WATER
3. WITH PEDAL POWER
5. ON THE TRACKS

DOWN

1. AT THE STATION
2. IN THE AIR
4. ON THE ROAD

PETS

ACROSS

1. BEGS FOR TREATS
5. EATS CRICKETS
7. NO LEGS AT ALL
8. HOPPITY

DOWN

2. BIG FURRY BALL OF LOVE
3. RODENT-LIKE CRITTER
4. CAN IMITATE HUMAN SPEECH
6. FELINE FRIEND

DAYS OF THE WEEK
NO CLUES!

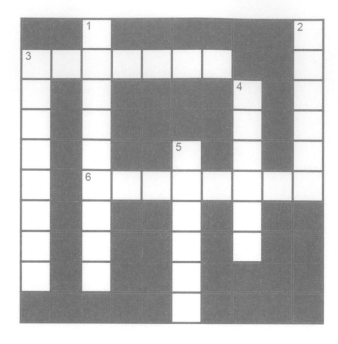

MONTHS OF THE YEAR
NO CLUES!

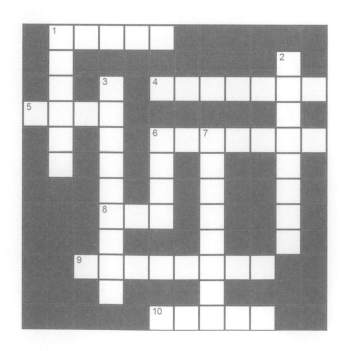

Cities of the Americas

THE CITIES BELOW CAN BE FOUND IN NORTH AND SOUTH AMERICA...AND IN THE WORD SEARCH PUZZLE BELOW. ANSWERS ON PAGE 91.

BOGOTÁ

BRASÍLIA

BUENOS AIRES

CARACAS

CHICAGO

DALLAS

GUADALAJARA

HOUSTON

LIMA

LOS ANGELES

MEXICO CITY

MIAMI

MONTREAL

NEW YORK

QUITO

RIO DE JANEIRO

SANTIAGO

SÃO PAULO

TORONTO

WASHINGTON

```
R I O D E J A N E I R O M Q C
L O S A N G E L E S L O E E A
F B L L S N U I K U A N X T R
H R M L A A N I T A O E I O A
S A T A O E O N X T I W C R C
C S P S P Y O P G M G Y O O A
H I A W N T B N A S J O C N S
I L Z N S F I I X U T R I T P
C I B U T H M I A I L K T O B
A A O O S I L J U L B O Y B O
G H A A J B A Q E X C C N R G
O U W X R X Z G O E L S F D O
M O N T R E A L O K R I C G T
G U A D A L A J A R A N M D A
Q B U E N O S A I R E S L A E
```

DEFINITION, NOT!

USUALLY WHEN TAKING A MULTIPLE-CHOICE TEST ONE OF THE POSSIBLE ANSWERS IS OBVIOUSLY INCORRECT. IT'S YOUR JOB HERE TO COME UP WITH THE OBVIOUSLY *WRONG* DEFINITION FOR THE FOLLOWING WORDS. FOR EXAMPLE, WE ALL KNOW A WILDFLOWER IS A FLOWER THAT GROWS UP IN THE WILD. HOWEVER, YOUR DEFINITION COULD BE: A PETUNIA IN A PLANE WITH A PARACHUTE OR A LION-TAMER LILY.

I'M A WILDFLOWER!

1. FIREWORKS

_____

2. MOUSETRAP

_____

3. SOFTBALL

_____

4. KEYBOARD

_____

5. REDHEAD

_____

 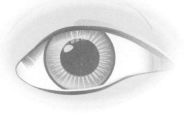

6. BUTTERFLY

_____

7. BACKBONE

_____

8. BABYSITTER

_____

9. HONEYMOON

_____

10. EYEBALL

_____

HAVE SOME TIME ON YOUR HANDS? SPELL "TIME" WITH YOUR HANDS! THIS IS THE AMERICAN SIGN LANGUAGE ALPHABET, WHICH IS THE MOST COMMON SIGN LANGUAGE OF DEAF COMMUNITIES IN THE UNITED STATES, PARTS OF CANADA, AND OTHER COUNTRIES AROUND THE WORLD. EACH HAND GESTURE REPRESENTS A LETTER OF THE ALPHABET. LEARN TO SIGN YOUR NAME. IF YOU WANT TO LEARN THE WHOLE ALPHABET, TEACH YOURSELF TO SIGN: "THE QUICK BROWN FOX JUMPS OVER THE LAZY DOG," WHICH IS A SENTENCE THAT CONTAINS EVERY LETTER OF THE ALPHABET AT LEAST ONCE.

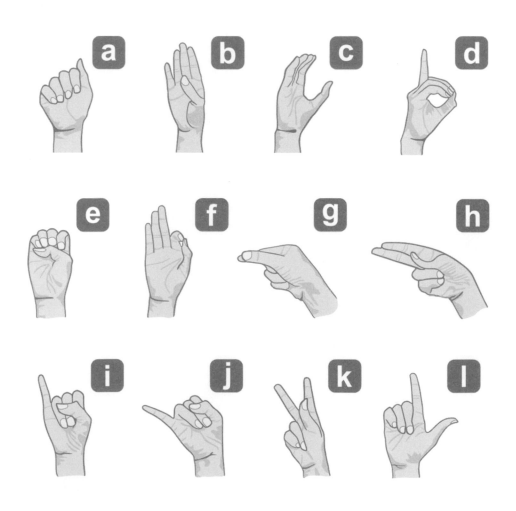

TiC-TaC-15

INSTEAD OF Xs AND Os, PLAY THE CLASSIC GAME WITH MATH. USING THE NUMBERS 1 THROUGH 9, TAKE TURNS TRYING TO GET A ROW TO EQUAL 15. EACH NUMBER CAN BE USED ONLY ONCE.

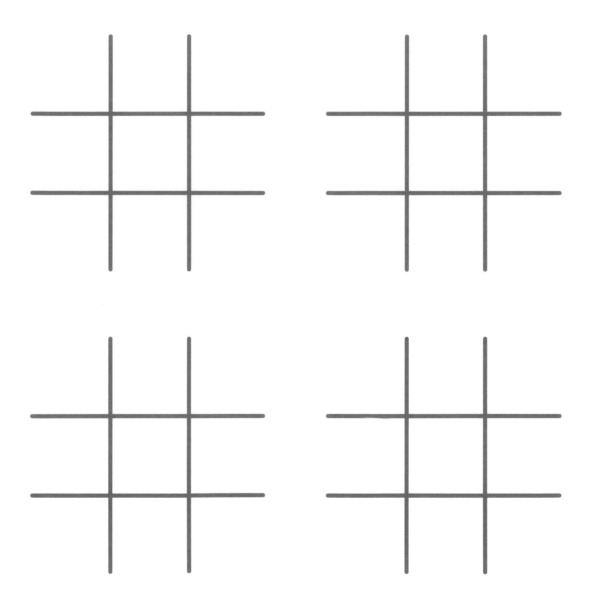

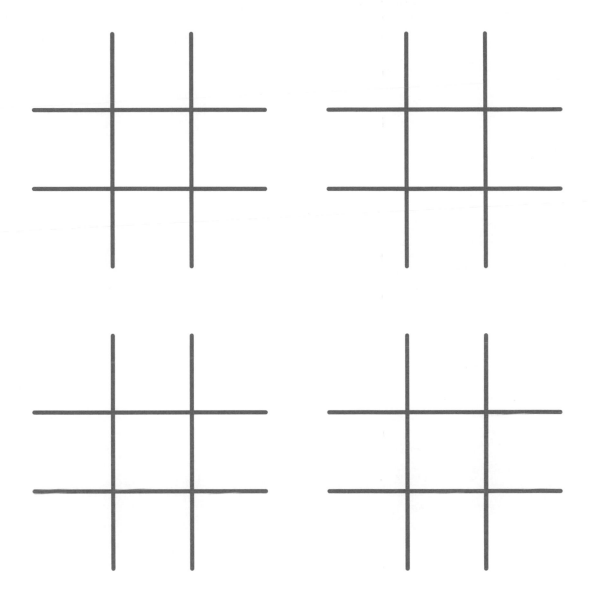

ONCE YOU'VE PLAYED A FEW TIMES, TRY THIS THIS OUT: FILL ONE OF THE TIC-TAC-TOE BOARDS ON THIS PAGE WITH THE NUMBERS 1 THROUGH 9, WITH NO NUMBER BEING USED TWICE. THE NUMBERS MUST ADD UP TO 15 IN ALL DIRECTIONS (HORIZONTALLY, VERTICALLY, AND DIAGONALLY). ANSWER ON PAGE 91.

THE TIME TRAVELER

FINISH THIS STORY. TURN THIS INTO A TAG-TEAM STORY BY GIVING EACH PERSON YOU ARE TRAVELING WITH THREE LINES EACH TO CONTINUE THE STORY. TAKE TURNS UNTIL THE STORY IS DONE.

WE HAD ONLY BEEN IN THE CAR FOR HALF AN HOUR AND MY LITTLE SISTER WAS ALREADY COMPLAINING THAT SHE HAD TO GO TO THE BATHROOM. WE WERE JUST OUTSIDE OF THE CITY LIMITS AND THE HIGHWAY HAD VERY LITTLE TRAFFIC. IN FACT, THE ONLY VEHICLE I SAW WAS A HORSE AND CARRIAGE. SUDDENLY IT DAWNED ON ME! WE WEREN'T TRAVELING THROUGH THE SUBURBS OF NEW JERSEY; WE WERE TRAVELING THROUGH TIME.

_____

_____

_____

_____

_____

_____

_____

_____

_____

_____

_____

_____

_____

Easy Sudoku

THIS IS A NUMBER-PLACING PUZZLE THAT'S USUALLY BASED ON A 9 X 9 GRID WITH SEVERAL GIVEN NUMBERS. THE OBJECT IS TO PLACE NUMBERS IN THE EMPTY SQUARES SO THAT EACH ROW, EACH COLUMN, AND EACH 3 X 3 BOX CONTAINS THE NUMBERS 1 TO 9 ONLY ONCE.

HINTS:

THE EASIEST WAY TO BEGIN SOLVING A SUDOKU PUZZLE IS TO START IN BOXES THAT ALREADY HAVE LOTS OF NUMBERS.

ANOTHER WAY IS TO SCAN ROWS AND COLUMNS, LOOKING FOR NUMBERS THAT CAN AND WON'T FIT. KEEP YOUR EYES OPEN FOR SITUATIONS WHERE ONLY ONE NUMBER CAN FIT IN A SINGLE SQUARE.

START OFF WITH THESE EASY 4 X 4 PUZZLES. THE NUMBERS 1, 2, 3, AND 4 CAN APPEAR IN EACH COLUMN, ROW AND 2 X 2 BOX ONLY ONCE. ANSWERS ON PAGE 91.

1.

1			
	2		3
			1
3			4

2.

3			1
			4
1		2	

3.

	3		2
			3
4			

4.

		2	
	3		
			4
	1		

5.

	3		
		4	
1	4		

6.

			4
2			
4	3		

7.

		6		4	
	3				
4	1		3	6	
	4				
5	2	3	4		
		5		3	

8.

		5			
3					5
				6	
		1	6		4
	6		2	1	3

9.

		4		6	
					1
	1		3		2
2	4				
					3
	2	5			

10.

3					
6		2		4	3
2		6	1		
		5			4
		4			6

11.

2	4			1	
	3	2			4
1	6		4		
		6		3	1
6			3	2	
	5			4	6

12.

				2	6
			5		
	1	2			
			2	5	1
					3
		6			

MORE DIFFICULT PUZZLES CAN BE FOUND ON PAGES 44 AND 80.

WORLD CiTiES

FIND 20 OF THE MOST INTERESTING CITIES IN THE WORLD IN THE WORD SEARCH BELOW. ANSWERS ON PAGE 92.

....

ALEXANDRIA   **MELBOURNE**   **SHANGHAI**

CAPE TOWN   **MEXICO CITY**   **TOKYO**

GENEVA   **MUMBAI**   **TORONTO**

JAKARTA   **NEW YORK**   **VENICE**

KHARTOUM   **ROME**   **VIENNA**

LONDON   **SÃO PAULO**   **ZURICH**

LOS ANGELES   **SEOUL**

```
C  S  A  O  P  A  U  L  O  K  O  M  O  G  F
A  A  J  K  Q  P  C  B  A  L  U  G  W  U  R
P  F  P  D  V  M  E  L  B  O  U  R  N  E  Z
C  M  B  E  K  E  L  L  T  S  P  B  X  B  B
T  E  Y  S  T  H  N  R  O  A  M  L  E  C  T
O  X  Z  H  T  O  A  I  P  N  D  B  F  Z  J
K  I  Q  A  R  H  W  C  C  G  D  O  L  D  A
Y  C  I  N  K  O  M  N  T  E  N  O  C  G  K
O  O  A  G  T  W  M  N  O  L  E  X  N  E  A
V  C  Y  H  U  H  U  E  R  E  W  F  V  N  R
F  I  J  A  C  M  M  J  O  S  Y  S  T  E  T
X  T  E  I  V  L  B  X  N  V  O  E  D  V  A
G  Y  R  N  H  T  A  O  T  N  R  O  A  A  T
O  U  F  V  N  B  I  F  O  Z  K  U  C  P  U
Z  A  L  E  X  A  N  D  R  I  A  L  B  Q  K
```

WiSH YOU WERE HERE!

SOMETIMES WHEN TRAVELING YOU HAVE TO LEAVE YOUR PETS WITH FRIENDS OR AT A KENNEL. WRITE A NOTE TO YOUR PET HERE, AND THEN ON THE FOLLOWING PAGE, IMAGINE WHAT YOUR PETS WOULD WRITE TO YOU ABOUT THEIR ADVENTURES WHILE YOU'RE AWAY.

DATE:

DEAR _____,

_____

_____

_____

_____

_____

_____

_____

_____

_____

_____

_____

_____

_____

_____

WITH LOVE,

_____

(SIGN YOUR NAME HERE)

ROBOT WORLD

DRAW WHAT THE FOLLOWING ITEMS WOULD LOOK LIKE IF THEY WERE ROBOTS.

· CHICKEN ·

· DOG ·

· FAN ·

· CAT ·

· TREE ·

· OCTOPUS ·

· AIRPLANE ·

· ELEPHANT ·

· GIRAFFE ·

LICENSE PLATE BINGO

THIS IS A FUN LICENSE PLATE GAME THAT IS PERFECT FOR LONG CAR RIDES.

1. GIVE EACH PLAYER IN THE CAR A GAME SHEET (SEE BELOW), OR A BLANK SHEET OF PAPER IN WHICH PLAYERS DRAW A 5 X 5 GRID.

2. HAVE AN ADULT CALL OUT RANDOM TWO-DIGIT NUMBER AND DOUBLE-LETTER COMBINATIONS, SUCH AS 58, 61, AB, ZF.

3. THE PLAYERS TAKE TURNS WRITING DOWN THE COMBINATIONS ON THEIR GAME CARDS UNTIL ALL THE BOXES ARE FILLED IN. (DON'T FORGET TO THANK THE ADULT FOR CALLING OUT ALL THOSE COMBOS!)

4. START HUNTING FOR THE COMBINATIONS ON YOUR BINGO CARDS. CROSS THEM OUT WHEN YOU FIND THEM AND CALL THEM OUT. YELL "BINGO" WHEN YOU HAVE A ROW, COLUMN, OR DIAGONAL CROSSED OFF. KEEP PLAYING UNTIL SOMEONE CROSSES OFF ALL THE BOXES IN THEIR GRID.

KNight Maze

CAN YOU HELP THE KNIGHT FIND HIS WAY TO THE PRINCESS? WATCH OUT FOR THE DRAGON! ANSWER ON PAGE 92.

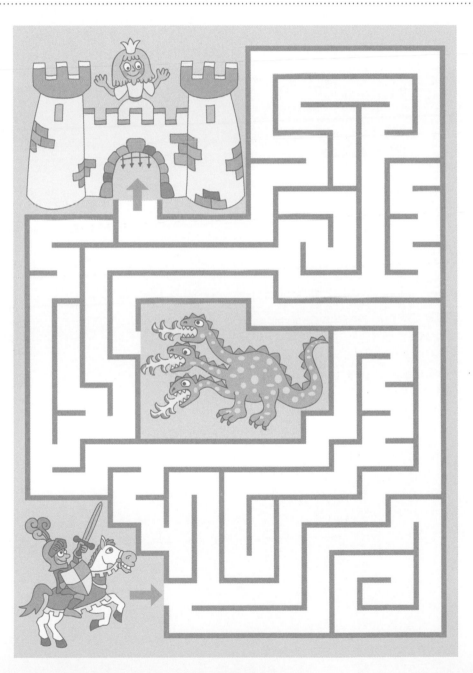

TAG-TEAM DRAWING

GET EVERYONE YOU'RE TRAVELING WITH (EXCEPT THE DRIVER OR PILOT) TO HELP CREATE A DRAWING. START OFF BY DRAWING A SQUIGGLE OR SIMPLE SHAPE. PASS THE PICTURE ALONG TO THE NEXT PERSON AND HAVE THEM ADD TO IT. KEEP PASSING IT AND ADDING STUFF UNTIL THE PAPER IS COVERED OR YOU CONCLUDE THAT YOU HAVE A MASTERPIECE.

BRAIN TICKLERS

TAKING AN AIRPLANE TO YOUR VACATION DESTINATION? TRY TO FIND THESE 20 ITEMS WHILE ON THE PLANE.

1. BARF BAG

2. IN-FLIGHT MAGAZINE

3. CHILD CRYING

4. PERSON SNORING

5. PERSON READING A TABLET

6. PERSON WITH SHOES OFF

7. THE PILOT!

8. A LAKE (LOOK OUT THE WINDOW!)

9. DARK CLOUDS

10. ANOTHER AIRPLANE

11. RED CARRY-ON BAG

12. MAN WITH A BEARD

13. WOMAN WITH A BLUE HAT

14. NECK PILLOW

15. AN EMPTY SEAT

16. PERSON TALKING LOUDLY

17. PERSON EATING FAST FOOD

18. MOUNTAINS (LOOK OUT WINDOW AGAIN!)

19. NO SMOKING SIGN

20. A BIRD

Vacation Time

USE THE CLUES TO FILL IN THE BLANKS. ANSWERS ON PAGE 92.

ACROSS
- 3. FISH ZOO
- 4. LOOPY RIDE (WITH 2 DOWN)
- 6. YOU NEED A ROD AND REEL TO DO THIS
- 7. USUALLY NEED 2 TO 4 PLAYERS AND DICE FOR THIS
- 11. TAKE A GUIDED _____
- 12. WHAT YOU DO IN 13 ACROSS
- 13. WHERE THE WATER IS
- 14. WHERE THE ART IS
- 16. WHERE THE OCEAN IS
- 17. WHAT YOU DO WHEN NO ONE WANTS TO COOK

DOWN
- 1. TAKE A _____.
- 2. SEE 4 ACROSS
- 5. WHAT YOU DO WITH MAGAZINES AND BOOKS
- 8. _____ PARK (WHERE YOU RIDE 4 ACROSS + 2 DOWN)
- 9. WHERE THE ANIMALS ARE
- 10. TWO-WHEELED, NON-MOTORIZED VEHICLE
- 12. WHAT YOU CATCH UP ON WHEN SUMMER VACATION STARTS
- 15. YOU WATCH IT WITH POPCORN

ALPHA BEASTS

TAKE THE FIRST LETTER OF ANY ANIMAL'S NAME AND CREATE THAT ANIMAL WITH IT!

CAT!

WORD CROSS

GRAB A FRIEND AND TRY THIS FUN GAME IN WHICH YOU END UP WITH A CROSSWORD PUZZLE. FIRST, CHOOSE A THEME, SUCH AS PEOPLE WE KNOW, ANIMALS, DESSERTS, FRUITS, AND TYPES OF CARS. THEN, DECIDE WHO GOES FIRST. THAT PLAYER THINKS OF A WORD THAT FITS INTO THE CATEGORY AND WRITES THE WORD IN THE GRID, ONE LETTER PER BOX. THE NEXT PLAYER THINKS OF ANOTHER WORD IN THAT CATEGORY, BUT IN ORDER TO PLACE IT IN THE GRID, THE WORD MUST SHARE A LETTER WITH THE WORD ALREADY ON THE GRID. KEEP DOING THIS UNTIL NO MORE WORDS CAN BE ADDED TO THE GRID. PLAYERS GET A POINT FOR EVERY LETTER THEY ADD TO THE GRID (NOT INCLUDING SHARED LETTERS). THE PLAYER WITH THE HIGHEST SCORE WINS. FOR A SIMPLER GAME, PLAY WITHOUT CHOOSING A CATEGORY. THAT WAY YOU CAN USE ANY WORD YOU THINK OF.

FINISH THIS WORD CROSS WITH MORE SALAD ITEMS!

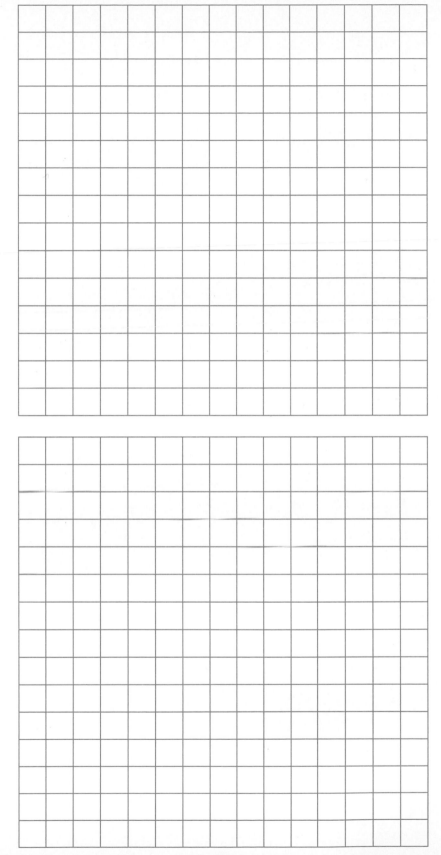

VOYAGE TO THE GREAT BEYOND

FINISH THIS STORY. TURN THIS INTO A TAG-TEAM STORY BY GIVING EACH PERSON YOU ARE TRAVELING WITH THREE LINES EACH TO CONTINUE THE STORY. TAKE TURNS UNTIL THE STORY IS DONE.

AS I FASTENED MY SEATBELT, I SAID TO MY TRAVELING COMPANIONS, "THIS SURELY ISN'T A NORMAL TRIP."

"NO, INDEED," SAID THE WOMAN WHO EVERYONE CALLED "CAPTAIN," BUT I CALLED "MOM."

"NOW, EVERYONE, PREPARE FOR A LONG NAP. OUR NEXT STOP IS 25 TRILLION MILES AWAY, PROXIMA CENTAURI."

I CLOSED MY EYES AND WE LIFTED OFF.

_____

_____

_____

_____

_____

_____

_____

_____

AFRICAN COUNTRIES

AFRICA IS THE WORLD'S SECOND LARGEST AND SECOND MOST POPULOUS
CONTINENT. THERE ARE 54 COUNTRIES IN AFRICA, OF WHICH YOU CAN FIND 20
BELOW. ANSWERS ON PAGE 92.

ALGERIA

BURKINA FASO

CAMEROON

EGYPT

ETHIOPIA

GHANA

KENYA

LIBYA

MADAGASCAR

MALI

MOROCCO

NIGERIA

RWANDA

SENEGAL

SOMALIA

SOUTH AFRICA

SUDAN

TANZANIA

UGANDA

ZIMBABWE

```
S H H E A C I R F A H T U O S
M O R O C C O L R C D P G Q J
T F E S E N E G A L L Y Y A D
E T H I O P I A C M A G X N P
Q O R A V Z V N S F C E H A E
D Q R J T A N Z A N I A A H Y
K U Z Y Y N I A G K D P I G P
E S R N A M D N A A X M L H N
N V C D B N P K D S L N A L O
Y B U A A A D N A W R L M R O
A S B G Y G J O M F G Z O Y R
G W U P B Y B U K E H Y S I E
E E P L I B N Q R N H Z Q C M
W W S X L T N I N I G E R I A
B U R K I N A F A S O E I J C
```

REST-STOP SCAVENGER HUNT

TAKING A BREAK FROM A LONG DRIVE AT A REST STOP? HOW MANY OF THE FOLLOWING ITEMS CAN YOU FIND BEFORE HITTING THE ROAD AGAIN?

1. PERSON WALKING A DOG

2. VENDING MACHINE

3. MAP

4. BROCHURE

5. AN RV

6. PERSON WITH A CANE

7. SOMEONE WITH A BROOM

8. OVERFLOWING GARBAGE CAN

9. LITTER (DON'T FORGET TO PICK IT UP!)

10. POOPER SCOOPER BAGS

11. CRYING BABY

12. BENCH

13. COFFEE VENDING MACHINE

14. WATER FOUNTAIN

15. "WELCOME" SIGN

16. ATM MACHINE

17. PICNIC TABLE

18. SOMEONE EMPTYING THEIR CAR OF TRASH

19. GRASS

20. CAR WITH AT LEAST TWO DOORS OPEN

BRAIN TICKLER SUDOKU

THIS IS A NUMBER-PLACING PUZZLE THAT'S USUALLY BASED ON A 9 X 9 GRID WITH SEVERAL GIVEN NUMBERS. THE OBJECT IS TO PLACE NUMBERS IN THE EMPTY SQUARES SO THAT EACH ROW, EACH COLUMN, AND EACH 3 X 3 BOX CONTAINS THE NUMBERS 1 TO 9 ONLY ONCE. IF THESE PUZZLES ARE TOO DIFFICULT, TURN TO PAGE 20 AND WORK ON THESE EASIER PUZZLES FIRST. ANSWERS ON PAGE 92.

1.

5		2	1			3	8	
	---	---	---	---	---	---	---	---
1		9					4	7
		8	6		3	1	5	
2	4					5	1	3
	8							
		7				9	2	
		5		7	4		9	
				6				
7			9				3	

2.

	7		5	3		2		
		2			1	5	4	
1			7	9	2		3	6
			4	8				5
		3				9	8	4
9	4		3			6		1
4		7						
2	3	9	6			4	5	

3.

				2			4	7
6					9		3	
2		4	3		6	1		
8			4	1	3	5	7	
3						4		1
7	4				8		2	6
		6	9	7	1			
	9		8			7	6	
5			6					2

4.

	6	1			5			
	3	4	9		6		2	
		9	1		4	3	6	5
	2		4					
8			6			2		
				7	2	8		
	9							6
		7				1	3	
4		8		6	7	5	9	

5.

		4		7		8		6
		8	9	3		4		
1		3	6			2		
	8	7		2		5		4
	5	6	3		7			8
9			8				2	
		2		6	3			
	6			9			1	
8		9	7					

6.

5				6			3	
2		8	5	9	4			
9			8					5
			6	3			2	
	5				9	1		
		2	7				6	
8	2		9			7	3	1
4	7		3	1	6		5	
	1	3						7

7.

			4			3		8
8			9		6	2		4
	1			2				5
2		7				4	8	
	5				4	6		9
4		8	1					
			5			9		
		5		6	9			3
6			8		2	1		

8.

		1			8			
	5	4				3		1
3	7	2		4		6		9
	4		9	7				2
6			8	1		7		
7	2	3			5	9		
2	8	7					4	5
5				8	4	2		
		6		5			8	3

Asian Cities

ASIA IS THE WORLD'S LARGEST AND MOST POPULOUS CONTINENT. ASIA HAS 48 COUNTRIES. YOU CAN FIND 20 OF ASIA'S MAJOR CITIES IN THE WORD SEARCH PUZZLE BELOW. ANSWERS ON PAGE 93.

BANGKOK

BEIJING

DUBAI

GUANGZHOU

HO CHI MINH CITY

HONG KONG

JAKARTA

KARACHI

KUALA LUMPUR

MANILA

MUMBAI

NEW DELHI

PHNOM PENH

PYONGYANG

SEOUL

SHANGHAI

SHENZHEN

TAIPEI

TEHRAN

TOKYO

```
Y A P J A K A R T A Y F Z P Z
T Q Q I A B U D N S P C P G K
I X A V M K U Z H D L S N U B
C P H N O M P E N H G I A I A
H Y J O H B N O M I U L R A N
N O I G V Z Y B A A A M H B G
I N Y O H K E H W L S E M K
M G W E O I G N U D G I T U O
I Y N T J N H M K I Z U L M K
H A L I A U P L K T H T U A R
C N N H X U W E E Z O A A R V
O G S D R Z E U V D U I S J L
H O N G K O N G C W W P P E O
J X I Z H T E V L U O E S T T
C X M K I K A R A C H I N I X
```

ARE WE THERE YET?

LONG CAR RIDES CAN BE BORING. FIND 12 THINGS TO DO IN THE CAR IN THIS WORD SEARCH PUZZLE. WORDS MAY BE HORIZONTAL, VERTICAL, DIAGONAL, FORWARD, OR BACKWARD. ANSWERS ON PAGE 93.

DRAW

LISTEN TO MUSIC

LOOK OUT WINDOW

NAP

PLAY A GAME

READ

SING

TALK

TEASE SIBLINGS

USE THIS BOOK

WATCH A VIDEO

WRITE

```
M C C G T N W F V R U X S J K
K C W H O T P O K Q C T Y R O
K L E O G E W E F O P E E L O
N E A G I N T D Z B W A G O B
U T V T O M H I E H D S C O S
P K M B I H R V R G V E G K I
G L C C O Q O A L W N S H O H
U N A A O V T H V W N I R U T
V B V Y X S V C P Y M B S T E
U H U S A P P T B N Y L F W S
Y K F L Z G J A Q D O I O I U
F K C K Z V A W W R V N R N J
P I P K Y N O M P A N G H D A
C H Z T U A W P E W S S U O H
L I S T E N T O M U S I C W B
```

Pack Your Bags!

TOMORROW YOU LEAVE FOR YOUR BIG VACATION! HAVE YOU PACKED YET? FIND THE FOLLOWING ITEMS IN THE WORD SEARCH BELOW, AND THEN MAKE SURE THEY'RE IN YOUR SUITCASE. ANSWERS ON PAGE 93.

BOOK
CAMERA
MAGAZINES
MAPS
PAJAMAS
PASSPORT
PILLOW
SANDALS
SNACKS
SUNGLASSES
SUNSCREEN
SWIMSUIT
TOOTHBRUSH
UMBRELLA
VIDEOS

```
N D L H A N N E E R C S N U S
I P I L L O W O C S A J S S A
A P Z Y L D B R B I J X O R S
X L J F E G P O D J R E E S W
U L S W R W O N G L D M E A D
D K W E B K V Q D I A V V N K
H G I S M D P F V C U H I D S
X B M H U W S E N I Z A G A M
P A S S P O R T U A Q W Y L A
Z T U W T S S A M A J A P S S
Z Y I J G R F P W T H G U K U
Q L T Y I H M B A M N B C E M
A A V H L D F Y L M S A C Z M
H S U R B H T O O T N O D W S
S O S S U N G L A S S E S I M
```

• 48 •

JUST HANGIN' AROUND MAZE

HELP THE GUY WITH THE LADDER FIND HIS WAY TO HIS POOR FRIEND BEFORE IT'S TOO LATE! ANSWER ON PAGE 93.

WORD SQUARES

CREATE AS MANY WORDS AS POSSIBLE INSIDE YOUR GRID!

1. GIVE EACH PLAYER A 4 X 4 GRID LIKE THE ONES ON THESE PAGES. RIP THEM OUT OR CREATE YOUR OWN ON SCRAP PAPER. TAKE TURNS NAMING A LETTER OF THE ALPHABET. PLAYERS CAN USE THE SAME LETTER MORE THAN ONCE. AS EACH LETTER IS CALLED OUT, EACH PLAYER MUST PLACE IT INSIDE HER GRID.

2. WHEN THE GRIDS ARE FULL, EACH PLAYER COUNTS THE NUMBER OF WORDS THEY WERE ABLE TO CREATE VERTICALLY, HORIZONTALLY, AND DIAGONALLY. THE PERSON WITH THE MOST WORDS, WINS.

HINT: YOU CAN CHOOSE LETTERS THAT HELP YOU COMPLETE WORDS, OR YOU CAN STOP YOUR OPPONENTS FROM GETTING WORDS BY CALLING OUT Q, X, AND OTHER UNCOMMON LETTERS.

NAME THE LAND MASS

ANSWERS ON PAGE 93.

1.

_____

2.

_____

3.

_____

4.

_____

5.

_____

6.

_____

7.

_____

8.

_____

9.

_____

10.

_____

11.

_____

12.

_____

THE "WHO ARE YOU?" GAME

HOW WELL DO YOU KNOW THE FAMILY MEMBERS OR FRIENDS YOU'RE TRAVELING WITH? AND HOW WELL DO THEY KNOW YOU? ANSWER THE QUESTIONS BELOW ABOUT ONE OF YOUR TRAVELING COMPANIONS. MEANWHILE, TEAR OUT THE NEXT PAGE AND HAVE THAT SAME PERSON ANSWER THE SAME QUESTIONS ABOUT YOU. THEN, ASK EACH OTHER THE QUESTIONS AND FILL IN THE RESPONSES. GIVE YOURSELF A POINT FOR EACH ANSWER YOU GUESSED CORRECTLY. WHO KNEW WHOM BETTER?

YOUR GUESS / ACTUAL ANSWER

1. WHAT'S YOUR FAVORITE COLOR? _____ / _____

2. WHAT ARE YOU MOST AFRAID OF? _____ / _____

3. WHAT'S YOUR FAVORITE GAME? _____ / _____

4. WHO IS YOUR HERO? _____ / _____

5. WHERE WOULD YOU MOST LIKE TO TRAVEL? _____ / _____

6. WHAT'S YOUR FAVORITE SNACK FOOD? _____ / _____

7. WHAT DO YOU WANT FOR YOUR NEXT BIRTHDAY? _____ / _____

8. WHAT'S YOUR FAVORITE MOVIE? _____ / _____

9. WHICH SUPERHERO WOULD YOU WANT TO BE? _____ / _____

10. IF YOU COULD BE A PRO ATHLETE, WHAT SPORT WOULD YOU PLAY? _____ / _____

1. WHAT'S YOUR FAVORITE COLOR? _____ / _____

2. WHAT ARE YOU MOST AFRAID OF? _____ / _____

3. WHAT'S YOUR FAVORITE GAME? _____ / _____

4. WHO IS YOUR HERO? _____ / _____

5. WHERE WOULD YOU MOST LIKE TO TRAVEL? _____ / _____

6. WHAT'S YOUR FAVORITE SNACK FOOD? _____ / _____

7. WHAT DO YOU WANT FOR YOUR NEXT BIRTHDAY? _____ / _____

8. WHAT'S YOUR FAVORITE MOVIE? _____ / _____

9. WHICH SUPERHERO WOULD YOU WANT TO BE? _____ / _____

10. IF YOU COULD BE A PRO ATHLETE, WHAT SPORT WOULD YOU PLAY? _____ / _____

THE GReat Storm

FINISH THIS STORY. TURN THIS INTO A TAG-TEAM STORY BY GIVING EACH PERSON YOU ARE TRAVELING WITH THREE LINES EACH TO CONTINUE THE STORY. TAKE TURNS UNTIL THE STORY IS DONE.

THE CRUISE VACATION PROMISED ALL THE GRANDEUR AND NONE OF THE DANGER OF THE ORIGINAL TITANIC VOYAGE. THE SHIP HAD EVERYTHING: A POOL, SEVERAL RESTAURANTS, A SMALL GOLF COURSE, AND A MOVIE THEATER. THERE WOULD BE NO FEAR OF ICEBERGS, THE BROCHURE SAID. HOWEVER, THE BROCHURE HAD NOTHING TO SAY ABOUT WHAT TO DO IF A MONSTER STORM WAS BARRELING TOWARD US, WHICH IS EXACTLY WHAT WAS HAPPENING AS MY BROTHER AND I JUMPED OUT OF THE POOL AND HEADED BACK TO OUR CABIN.

_____

_____

_____

_____

_____

_____

_____

_____

_____

HOW MANY _____ CAN YOU NAME?

U.S. STATES

_____

_____

_____

_____

_____

_____

COUNTRIES OF THE WORLD

_____

_____

_____

_____

_____

_____

EUROPEAN COUNTRIES

_____

_____

_____

_____

_____

SOUTH AMERICAN COUNTRIES

_____
_____
_____
_____
_____
_____

AFRICAN COUNTRIES

_____
_____
_____
_____
_____
_____

WORLD CITIES

_____
_____
_____
_____
_____
_____

TOO-CLOSE-FOR-COMFORT GAMES

TRAVELING USUALLY MEANS BEING SQUISHED TOGETHER IN A CAR, PLANE, OR TRAIN. HERE ARE SOME GAMES YOU CAN PLAY SITTING DOWN WITH A SEATBELT ON.

ABC GAMES

THIS IS A GREAT GAME FOR A LONG, BORING CAR TRIP. YOU CAN PLAY IT ALONE OR WITH WHOEVER ELSE IS IN THE CAR. THE GOAL IS TO FIND OBJECTS OUT YOUR WINDOW THAT BEGIN WITH THE LETTERS OF THE ALPHABET ... IN ALPHABETICAL ORDER. FOR INSTANCE: A...AUTOMOBILE, B...BIRD, C...CAB, AND SO ON. THE FIRST PERSON TO GET TO Z WINS.

OR HAVE A CONVERSATION WITH A TRAVEL MATE IN WHICH EACH SENTENCE MUST START WITH A DIFFERENT LETTER OF THE ALPHABET, IN CONSECUTIVE ORDER FROM A TO Z.

THE GUESSING GAME?

THIS GAME IS FOR TWO PLAYERS. EACH PERSON SECRETLY WRITES DOWN ANY NUMBER FROM 1 TO INFINITY. YOU SHOW EACH OTHER THE NUMBERS YOU WROTE, AND THE PERSON WITH THE LOWER NUMBER WINS 1 POINT.... UNLESS SOMEONE CHOOSES A NUMBER 1 GREATER THAN THE OTHER PERSON. IN THAT CASE, THAT PERSON RECEIVES 2 POINTS. WHOEVER SCORES 50 POINTS FIRST WINS.

SEAT CHARADES

THIS IS LIKE THE REAL GAME OF CHARADES, EXCEPT YOU CAN ONLY USE YOUR HANDS AND FACIAL EXPRESSIONS.

MY CAR

EACH PASSENGER CHOOSES A COLOR AND A BRAND OF CAR. FOR INSTANCE: RED FORD OR YELLOW CHEVY. ONCE EVERYONE HAS CHOSEN, BE ON THE LOOKOUT FOR YOUR CARS. WHOEVER HAS THE MOST AT THE END OF THE TRIP WINS.

CONNECT THE WORDS

THE DRIVER SAYS A WORD. SUCH AS: *ENVELOPE*. THE PERSON IN THE PASSENGER SEAT HAS TO COME UP WITH A WORD THAT STARTS WITH THE SAME SOUND THAT THE PREVIOUS WORD ENDED WITH: *OPENER*. THE NEXT PLAYER CONTINUES: *NERVOUSLY*...AND SO ON UNTIL YOU'RE STUMPED.

CHOOSE A COLOR

HAVE THE DRIVER CHOOSE A COLOR. EVERYONE ELSE LOOKS AROUND TO FIND 5 THINGS OF THAT COLOR EITHER INSIDE OR OUTSIDE THE CAR. THE FIRST PERSON TO NAME FIVE ITEMS WINS. YOU CAN DECIDE TO CHOOSE A LETTER INSTEAD OF A COLOR AND FIND THINGS THAT BEGIN ... OR END! ... WITH THAT LETTER.

GNILLEPS EEB

TAKE TURNS GIVING EACH OTHER WORDS TO SPELL. HOWEVER, YOU HAVE TO SPELL THE WORDS BACKWARD...WITHOUT WRITING THEM DOWN!

FINGER MESSAGE

HAVE ONE TRAVELER CLOSE HER EYES WHILE SOMEONE ELSE WRITES A MESSAGE IN THE PALM OF HER HAND. CAN SHE GUESS IT? TAKE TURNS AND SEE WHO'S BEST AT DECIPHERING THE FINGER MESSAGES.

TIME FLIES

SET THE TIMER ON A SMARTPHONE FOR ONE MINUTE. CHOOSE A TIME KEEPER, WHO WILL TELL EVERYONE WHEN TO CLOSE THEIR EYES. AS THE TIME KEEPER KEEPS TRACK OF ONE FULL MINUTE, EVERYONE ELSE TRIES TO GUESS HOW LONG A MINUTE IS. WHEN A PLAYER THINKS A MINUTE IS PASSED, SHE OPENS HER EYES. THE TIME KEEPER MARKS THE TIME EACH PLAYER'S EYES OPENED. THE PLAYER WHO'S GUESSED CLOSEST TO ONE MINUTE WINS.

WHAT'S DIFFERENT?

HAVE YOUR SEAT MATE LOOK CAREFULLY AT YOU, TRYING TO MEMORIZE THE DETAILS OF YOUR APPEARANCE. THEN HE CLOSES HIS EYES. YOU, MEANWHILE, HAVE TO CHANGE ONE THING ABOUT YOUR APPEARANCE. IF YOUR COLLAR WAS DOWN, PUT IT UP; ARRANGE YOUR HAIR DIFFERENTLY; UNBUTTON A BUTTON; TAKE OFF A BRACELET. WHEN YOU'RE DONE, TELL YOUR PARTNER TO OPEN HIS EYES. SEE IF HE CAN GUESS WHAT CHANGED. TAKE TURNS.

EXPERTS

PICK AN EXPERT AND TWO QUESTIONERS. THE QUESTIONERS SECRETLY PICK A TOPIC THAT THE EXPERT SUPPOSEDLY KNOWS EVERYTHING ABOUT. THEN THEY ASK THE EXPERT QUESTIONS, AND THE EXPERT HAS TO GUESS WHAT SHE'S AN EXPERT IN BASED ON THE QUESTIONS.

CASTAWAYS

PRETEND YOUR WHOLE FAMILY (OR WHOEVER YOU'RE TRAVELING WITH) IS TRAVELING TO A COMPLETELY UNINHABITED ISLAND FOR A THREE-WEEK STAY. HOWEVER, YOUR FAMILY CAN ONLY BRING FIVE THINGS WITH YOU (NOT FIVE THINGS EACH BUT FIVE THINGS ALTOGETHER). DISCUSS WHAT YOU WILL BRING AND VOTE ON THE LIST. CAN YOU ALL AGREE 100% ON A LIST?

AROUND-THE-DiaL SCaVENGER HuNT

CHALLENGING

PLAY THIS GAME WITH EVERYONE IN THE CAR! HAVE THE FRONT-SEAT PASSENGER TURN THE RADIO DIAL AND HAVE EVERYONE LISTEN FOR THE FOLLOWING. CIRCLE EVERYTHING YOU "FIND."

1. TAYLOR SWIFT SONG

2. A COUGH

3. TWO PEOPLE LAUGHING

4. SPORTS TALK

5. BEATLES SONG

6. OPERA

7. CLASSICAL VIOLIN

8. SILLY SOUND EFFECT

9. SONG WITH NO WORDS

10. AD FOR USED CARS

11. WEATHER ALERT TEST

12. RADIO CALL LETTERS

13. RUNNING WATER

14. AD FOR A DRUG WITH A LOT OF SIDE EFFECTS

15. A CALL-IN PROGRAM

16. MUSIC COUNTDOWN

17. SONG ABOUT A BROKEN HEART

18. SONG IN A FOREIGN LANGUAGE (TO YOU)

19. A CONTEST IN WHICH YOU HAVE TO CALL IN TO THE STATION TO WIN

20. TRAFFIC UPDATE

CIRCLE UP

CAN YOU GET TO THE CENTER OF THINGS WITH THESE THREE MAZES? ANSWERS ON PAGE 93.

WORD DRAWINGS

CREATE WORD DRAWINGS OF THE FOLLOWING ITEMS. INSTEAD OF DRAWING SHAPES FOR THE DIFFERENT PARTS, YOU ARE USING THE *NAMES* OF THE DIFFERENT PARTS. FOR INSTANCE, IF YOU'RE DRAWING A FLOWER, INSTEAD OF DRAWING PETALS, YOU WRITE THE WORD PETAL WHEREVER YOU WANT ONE. THEN YOU WRITE THE WORD "STEM" VERTICALLY FOR ITS STEM, AND SO ON. BE AS DETAILED AS YOU WANT.

TRY IT!

· CAR ·

· CAT ·

· HUMAN ·

· HOUSE ·

· LIVING ROOM ·

· ROBOT ·

· MAP OF THE WORLD ·

DOUBLE LETTERS

FILL IN THE BLANKS WITH THE LETTERS THAT COMPLETE
THE WORDS. ANSWERS ON PAGE 94.

1. EATS ANTS

A A_ _ _ _ _ _

2. GIFT WRAPPING

_ _ B B _ _

3. YOU DID IT!

_ _ C C _ _ _

4. WHERE YOU LIVE

_ D D _ _ _ _

5. WHAT YOU STAND ON

_ E E _

6. WHEN A ROCKET LEAVES

_ _ _ _ _ F F

7. WHEN YOU THROW AND CATCH THREE
BALLS

_ _ G G _ _

8. GET A RIDE FROM A STRANGER

_ _ _ _ _ H H _ _ _

9. SLIDING DOWN A WINTRY HILL

_ _ I I _ _

10. TRAVELED

_ _ _ K K _ _

11. _____ OR NOTHING

_ L L

12. ALL WRAPPED UP

_ _ M M _

13. NOT A LOSER

_ _ N N _ _

14. TAKE OFF YOUR SHOES

_ _ _ _ _ O O _

15. FRUIT FOR PIE

_ P P _ _

16. ORANGE ROOT VEGETABLE

_ _ R R _ _

17. WHAT A BUTTON TELLS YOU TO DO

_ _ _ S S

18. BABY FELINE

_ _ T T _ _

19. SUCKS UP DIRT

_ _ _ U U _

20. DROVE AT HIGH SPEED

_ _ V V _ _

21. WHAT THE DOG SAYS

_ _ W W _ _

22. CHEESE, SAUCE, BREAD

_ _ Z Z _

WORD JUMBLES

UNSCRAMBLE THE WORDS IN EACH PUZZLE, AND THEN USE THE SHADED LETTERS TO FORM A WORD THAT IS THE PUNCHLINE OF THE JOKES. USE THE EMPTY SPACE ON THE PAGES TO FIGURE OUT THE WORDS. ONE TRICK IS TO PLACE ALL THE LETTERS OF A SCRAMBLED WORD IN A CIRCLE. FOR EXAMPLE, THE LETTERS LBWEO MAY BE DIFFICULT TO SORT OUT, BUT WHEN PLACED LIKE THIS:

```
        W
      B   L
      E   O
```

IT'S EASIER TO SEE THE WORD IS "ELBOW." ANSWERS ON PAGE 94.

1. WHERE DO COWS GO ON VACATION? _____
   JUMBLE HINT: FIRST NAMES

   A) AMRK
   B) OOZYE
   C) OYR

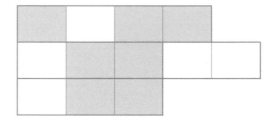

2. WHERE DO SHARKS GO ON VACATION? _____
   JUMBLE HINT: U.S. STATES

   A) LRFODAI
   B) AHODI
   C) WEN RKYO
   D) ERNABKSA

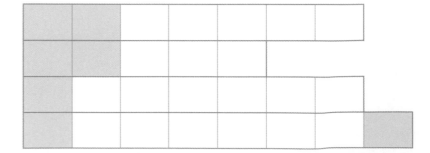

3. WHERE DO SHEEP GO ON VACATION? _____
   JUMBLE HINT: SCHOOL SUPPLIES

   A) CBAPCKAK
   B) NUOCHBXL
   C) ERRASE
   D) ERMKRAS

4. WHY DID THE ROBOT GO ON VACATION? HE NEEDED TO _____ HIS
   BATTERIES.
   JUMBLE HINT: FRUIT

   A) PAEPL
   B) RONAEG
   C) PRGAES
   D) EHRYCR

5. WHAT DID THE PIECE OF BREAD DO ON VACATION? _____ AROUND!
   JUMBLE HINT: ANIMALS

   A) LONI
   B) OIBSN
   C) OGLDIFHS
   D) EBZAR

6. WHERE DID SUSAN GO ON VACATION? I DON'T KNOW, _____!
   JUMBLE HINT: SPORTS

   A) ASBELALB
   B) KISING
   C) OTBFAOLL

DESiGNER PLatES

CREATE LICENSE PLATES FOR YOUR FAVORITE PLACES.

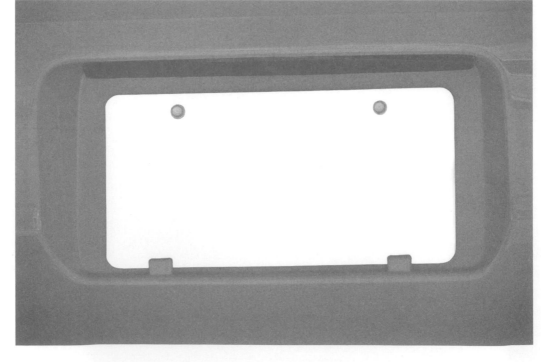

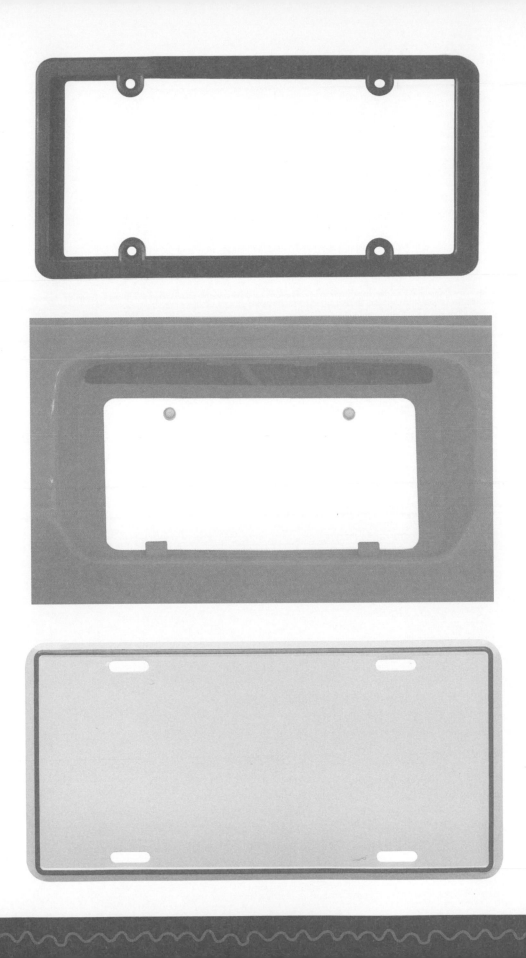

RHYME TiME

YOU'RE GOING ON VACATION, BUT YOU'RE NOT THERE YET. MAYBE THE CAR RIDE IS STARTING TO BOTHER YOU. NARRATE WHAT'S GOING ON IN THE CAR, PLANE, OR BOAT WITH LITTLE TWO-LINE RHYMES. FOR INSTANCE:

"MY LITTLE BROTHER, HIS NAME IS JOE.

WE JUST STARTED DRIVING AND HE HAS TO GO."

OR

"THE CAR JUST PASSED US DOING 95.

I DON'T THINK HE SHOULD BE ALLOWED TO DRIVE."

_____

_____

_____

_____

_____

_____

_____

_____

_____

NAME THE TOURIST ATTRACTIONS

...AND WHERE THEY ARE LOCATED! ANSWERS ON PAGE 94.

1.

_____

_____

2.

_____

_____

3.

_____

_____

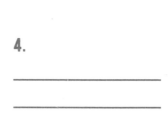

4.

_____

_____

5.

_____

_____

6.

_____

_____

7.

_____

_____

8.

_____

_____

9.

_____

_____

10.

_____

_____

11.

_____

_____

12.

_____

_____

CHALLENGING SUDOKU

THIS IS A NUMBER-PLACING PUZZLE THAT'S USUALLY BASED ON A 9 X 9 GRID WITH SEVERAL GIVEN NUMBERS. THE OBJECT IS TO PLACE NUMBERS IN THE EMPTY SQUARES SO THAT EACH ROW, EACH COLUMN, AND EACH 3 X 3 BOX CONTAINS THE NUMBERS 1 TO 9 ONLY ONCE. IF THESE PUZZLES ARE TOO DIFFICULT, TURN TO PAGE 20 OR PAGE 44 AND WORK ON THESE EASIER SUDOKU PUZZLES FIRST. ANSWERS ON PAGE 94.

1.

5			6					8
						4		
	1	8		3				7
		1		2		8		
	7					6	5	
				8				
		4			5			
			1		2			
6			2	7		1		

2.

5		4	8					
			5		9			
	1			4				
		9				4		
2								
	8			1			3	7
9				5				
		8	2				5	
		3	1			7		6

3.

			5		1	6	7	
		5			8			
				7	2	8		1
		3	8					
7								
8					6	4		
								6
	2				1	5		
9					3	1		8

THESE TWO PUZZLES USE THE LETTERS A THROUGH I INSTEAD OF 1 THROUGH 9.
YOU SOLVE IT THE SAME AS A NUMBER SUDOKU.

4.

	G	I	C	E				
		A						
H			G					
			B	F			E	
	F			G				D
			I			B	C	
		F	E				B	
			A			I	G	
E	A							

5.

C				D		E	G	
	E						I	A
D		I	E		A		C	H
	G		A		C		B	
I		C						G
	A	D		I			F	
F				D				E
	D	E	C	F	I		H	B
B		H						I

THIS IS THE MOST DIFFICULT SUDOKU IN THIS BOOK!

6.

1								
8	7			3	6			
5	2				9		7	
							1	
				2	3		4	
7			4					9
	1		9					7
4								6
6			7		1		5	4

Vanity Plates

DECIDE WHICH OF THESE PERSONALIZED LICENSE PLATES BELONGS TO WHOM. FOR INSTANCE, A DENTIST MIGHT HAVE A VANITY PLATE THAT READS: 2TH AKE (TOOTHACHE). ANSWERS ON PAGE 94.

1. JEALOUS PERSON	EDUC8R
2. HOCKEY PLAYER	N4CER
3. SOMEONE WITH GOOD EYESIGHT	W8R
4. IMPATIENT PERSON	U4IC
5. PERSON HAPPY WITH HIMSELF	HD DR
6. OVERWHELMINGLY HAPPY PERSON	BO K
7. ANOTHER REALLY HAPPY PERSON	2M80
7. ELECTRICIAN	I M NVS
8. COMEDIAN WHO DOES VOICES	SHRTCRCT
9. GARBAGE COLLECTOR	ISK8
10. BASEBALL PITCHER	H82W8
11. FARMER	GR82BME
12. FLOWER SHOP OWNER	IC 2020
13. PSYCHIATRIST	N XTC
14. FOOD SERVER	IMTCANS
15. POLICE OFFICER	IMIT8
16. TEACHER	STRYK3

Backward & Forward

THE FOLLOWING SENTENCES HAVE TWO MISSING WORDS. FILL THE BLANKS IN EACH SENTENCE WITH A WORD AND THEN ITS MIRROR WORD, WHICH IS THE FIRST WORD SPELLED BACKWARD. ANSWERS ON PAGE 94.

....

EXAMPLE:
STEVE WANTED TO JUMP <u>ON</u> THE MATTRESS, BUT HIS MOM SAID <u>NO</u>.

....

1. ANITA HAD HER _____ TESTED _____ FOUND OUT SHE WAS OF GERMAN AND ITALIAN ANCESTRY.

2. PUPPIES ARE GREAT _____, BUT MAKE SURE YOU DON'T _____ ON THEM!

3. IT TOOK ME _____ TRIES TO GET THE BALL OVER THE _____.

4. THE _____ OF LEFTOVER SAUCE IS ON THE _____ SHELF OF THE REFRIGERATOR.

5. ADRIAN SWAM A FULL _____ IN THE OLYMPIC-SIZED _____.

6. MARCIA FILLED THE _____, _____ THE WATER WAS WAY TOO HOT.

7. WHEN SILVIA IS IN A BAD _____, IT'S ALL _____ AND GLOOM.

8. _____ MISSED THE EXIT AND HAD TO PULL OVER TO CONSULT A _____.

9. LEO _____ THE MORNING WITH NOTHING BUT A CUP OF _____ COFFEE.

10. DAD WANTS TO KNOW WHO STUCK A PIECE OF _____ TO HIS COFFEE _____.

11. _____ SPIRITS _____ IN THE HAUNTED HOUSE.

12. HE _____ YESTERDAY'S CHESS MATCH, BUT HE'S LOSING _____.

THINGS WE SAY IN THE CAR

CAN YOU FIND 10 COMMON PHRASES WE ALL SAY WHEN TRAVELING IN THE CAR? NO CLUES! ANSWERS ON PAGE 95.

```
S O M E T H I N G S M E L L S
V Y Z Q G I F C U E Q G X H T
B W O T O Q C D E F X M E T W
M E H I P M Q P Y A O R E B I
J R F O M T O V H B E Y P G M
C Y I R T T A W B H E R A S B
J R N G E E H K O R Q G Z L O
N Q X V L U T I E K M N N O R
I R A K B E T H R A U I M W E
P H B S Y O T S T S N Z K D D
I G T F H E N T T E T A P O L
X X J S W T R C A V C Y P W S
T Y T E I M H U N G R Y X N K
X I R G O A G B J Z D F O K H
C A N I S I T U P F R O N T A
```

Out the Window

HERE'S A CROSSWORD WHERE EVERY ANSWER IS SOMETHING YOU MAY SEE OUTSIDE YOUR CAR WINDOW. ANSWERS ON PAGE 95.

ACROSS

2 FILL 'ER UP
5 PUFFY THINGS YOU SEE WHEN YOU LOOK UP
6 HALT WHEN YOU SEE THIS
10 UNFORTUNATE FLAT ANIMAL
11 TRASH
12 MOO
13 WHERE YOU GO WHEN YOU NEED A BREAK

DOWN

1 SOMEONE WHO WANTS A RIDE
3 IT LEAVES A CONTRAIL IN THE SKY
4 OPPOSITE OF SLOW EATS
7 LOTS OF CARS GOING NOWHERE
8 THEY CHECK FOR SPEEDING
9 18-WHEELER

TRAVEL PHOBIAS

A PHOBIA IS AN EXTREME OR IRRATIONAL FEAR OF SOMETHING. FOR EXAMPLE, AN IRRATIONAL FEAR OF SPIDERS IS CALLED ARACHNOPHOBIA. CAN YOU FIGURE OUT THE DEFINITIONS OF THE PHOBIAS IN THE FOLLOWING PARAGRAPHS? ANSWERS ON PAGE 95.

IN THE CAR

I'M SQUISHED INTO THE BACKSEAT OF THE SMALL CAR WITH MY TWO SIBLINGS AND SUFFERING FROM (1) CLAUSTROPHOBIA. MEANWHILE, MY DAD'S (2) VEHOPHOBIA HAS KICKED IN SO MY MOM HAS TO DO ALL THE DRIVING. MY BROTHER BREATHES FROM HIS MOUTH AND HAS TO KEEP A WINDOW OPEN BECAUSE OF HIS (3) OSMOPHOBIA, AND MY SISTER WON'T FALL ASLEEP BECAUSE OF HER (4) ONEIROPHOBIA.

ON AN AIRPLANE

MR. BURNS DECIDED TO TAKE HIS WHOLE FAMILY TO THE BAHAMAS FOR A VACATION GETAWAY. THE WHOLE FAMILY TOOK AN AIRPLANE, EXCEPT FOR COUSIN BETSY, WHO HAS (5) ACROPHOBIA. MRS. BURN REFUSED TO SIT NEXT TO A YOUNG FAMILY DUE TO HER (6) PEDOPHOBIA. COUSIN BEN FREAKED OUT WHEN THE PILOT SAID TO TURN OFF ALL CELLPHONES BECAUSE OF HIS (7) NOMOPHOBIA. AUNT SUSAN WORE RUBBER GLOVES BECAUSE OF HER (8) MYSOPHOBIA. AND FINALLY, MR. BURNS, HIMSELF, REFUSED TO TALK TO ANYONE IN HIS ROW BECAUSE OF HIS (9) HALITOPHOBIA.

IN A BOAT

LUCY, DESPITE HER (10) AQUAPHOBIA, DECIDED TO TRAVEL TO EUROPE BY BOAT. THIS WAS A HUGE MISTAKE BECAUSE ONCE ONBOARD, SHE REALIZED SHE COULDN'T LOOK AT THE WATER BECAUSE OF HER (11) ICHTHYOPHOBIA. SHE ALSO COULDN'T SPEND ANYTIME ON DECK WITH THE OTHER PASSENGERS BECAUSE OF HER (12) ANTHROPOPHOBIA.

ON A TRAIN

TAKING THE TRAIN WAS NOT A GOOD IDEA FOR SIMON. HE DIDN'T KNOW HE SUFFERED FROM (13) SIDERODROMOPHOBIA UNTIL THE TRAIN LEFT THE STATION. WHILE CROSSING A RIVER, HE LEARNED OF HIS (14) GEPHYROPHOBIA. HE HAD TO LEAVE THE THIRTEENTH CAR BECAUSE OF HIS (15) TRISKAIDEKAPHOBIA.

NO MATTER THEIR FEARS, EACH TRAVELER ON THESE PAGES MADE IT SAFELY TO THEIR DESTINATION AND, IN FACT, STAYED LONGER THAN ANTICIPATED BECAUSE OF THEIR (16) NOSTOPHOBIA!

1. _____
2. _____
3. _____
4. _____
5. _____
6. _____
7. _____
8. _____
9. _____
10. _____
11. _____
12. _____
13. _____
14. _____
15. _____
16. _____

· FUN FACTS! ·

SCARED OF DECIDING WHICH WAY TO TRAVEL? YOU MAY HAVE DECIDOPHOBIA, WHICH IS THE FEAR OF MAKING DECISIONS.

IF YOU'RE SCARED OF ALL THIS FEAR, YOU MAY HAVE PHOBOPHOBIA, WHICH IS A FEAR OF FEAR.

COMPOUND WORDS

WHAT WORD WILL FIT IN FRONT OF THE FOLLOWING GROUPS OF WORDS TO FORM NEW WORDS? ANSWERS ON PAGE 95.

....

1. _____ HEART
NESS
BREAD
PEA

5. _____ BED
PROOF
COLORS
FOWL

2. _____ KERCHIEF
LACE
TIE
BAND

6. _____ BLOCK
BATHE
BURST
BURN

3. _____ ONE
DAY
BODY
PLACE

7. _____ ACHE
BOARD
BONE
DROP

4. _____ PLANT
DOWN
MASK
LIFT

8. _____ PAD
BOARD
HOLE
WORD

9. _____ BALL
MAN
FLAKE
BANK

13. _____ DISH
STONE
BOX
SUDS

10. _____ MISTRESS
QUARTERS
DRESS
PHONES

14. _____ PEN
LET
TAIL
SKIN

11. _____ SHAKE
WRITING
CUFF
BAG

15. _____ NIP
NAP
TAIL
FIGHT

12. _____ BRAND
BALL
FIGHTER
PROOF

16. _____ BIRD
BERRY
BELL
FISH

EUROPEAN CITIES

EUROPE BOASTS 50 COUNTRIES (A FEW OF WHICH ARE IN BOTH ASIA AND EUROPE). YOU CAN FIND 20 EUROPEAN CITIES BELOW. ANSWERS ON PAGE 95.

```
B P M A D R E T S M A A M W N
M R U E E V M W A R S A W H I
N A L I M M N H Z B D D T V K
T G W O C S O M A R U Y I H N
C U Y Y M X T R I B R E F A I
O E I C O B C D L Z N E W M S
P I O F W E G I S N E H T A L
E B W S L R N R A O C Z Z A D
N U K O C G B K W D E B A R H
H D N S Z A T O I N I L R E B
A A I B A Z L Q O O C M O T J
G P R L G H W R U L O L J T Z
E E Y M C Z S N E D S Q Q O S
N S B W V N X R Z O G T P R D
P T K C P Y D S W V P A R I S
```

AMSTERDAM	COPENHAGEN	MILAN	ROME
ATHENS	DUBLIN	MOSCOW	ROTTERDAM
BARCELONA	HELSINKI	OSLO	VIENNA
BERLIN	LONDON	PARIS	WARSAW
BUDAPEST	MADRID	PRAGUE	ZAGREB

ANSWERS

MINI CROSSWORDS ANSWERS (PAGE 8)

THE NOISES ANIMALS MAKE

```
M E O W
  I
  N E I G H
B A R K   I
  O       S
Q U A C K S
  R
```

GETTING AROUND

```
    B O A T
    U   I
    S   R
        P
B I C Y C L E
    A     A
  T R A I N E
```

BUGS THAT BOTHER

```
A       M
N       O
T I C K S   B
S       Q   E
    F L I E S
      L I
      E O
      A E
W A S P S
```

PETS

```
    D O G
H   U   P
A   L I Z A R D
M   C N   R
S N A K E   R
T   T A   O
E     P   T
R A B B I T
      G
```

DAYS OF THE WEEK

```
      W         M
T U E S D A Y   O
H   D       F   N
U   N       R   D
R   E     S I   A
S   S A T U R D A Y
D   D     N A Y
A   A     D Y
Y   Y     A
          Y
```

MONTHS OF THE YEAR

```
A P R I L
U       F
G   S O C T O B E R
J U N E       B
U   P   J A N U A R Y
S   T   U   O   U
T   E   L   V   A
    M A Y   E   R
    B       M   Y
    D E C E M B E R
    R       E
      M A R C H
```

CITIES OF THE AMERICAS ANSWERS (PAGE 11)

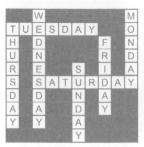

TIC-TAC-15 ANSWER (PAGE 17)

6	1	8
7	5	3
2	9	4

EASY SUDOKU ANSWERS (PAGE 20)

1.

1	3	4	2
4	2	1	3
2	4	3	1
3	1	2	4

2.

3	2	4	1
4	1	3	2
2	3	1	4
1	4	2	3

3.

1	3	4	2
2	4	1	3
3	1	2	4
4	2	3	1

4.

1	4	2	3
2	3	4	1
3	2	1	4
4	1	3	2

5.

4	3	2	1
2	1	4	3
1	4	3	2
3	2	1	4

6.

3	1	2	4
2	4	3	1
4	3	1	2
1	2	4	3

7.

2	5	6	1	4	3
6	3	4	5	2	1
4	1	2	3	6	5
3	4	1	6	5	2
5	2	3	4	1	6
1	6	5	2	3	4

8.

6	1	5	4	3	2
3	2	6	1	4	5
4	5	2	3	6	1
2	3	1	6	5	4
1	4	3	5	2	6
5	6	4	2	1	3

9.

1	3	4	2	6	5
6	5	2	4	3	1
5	1	6	3	4	2
2	4	3	1	5	6
4	6	1	5	2	3
3	2	5	6	1	4

10.

3	5	1	4	6	2
4	2	3	6	5	1
6	1	2	5	4	3
2	4	6	1	3	5
1	6	5	3	2	4
5	3	4	2	1	6

11.

2	4	5	6	1	3
5	3	2	1	6	4
1	6	3	4	5	2
4	2	6	5	3	1
6	1	4	3	2	5
3	5	1	2	4	6

12.

5	3	1	4	2	6
6	2	3	5	1	4
4	1	2	6	3	5
3	6	4	2	5	1
2	4	5	1	6	3
1	5	6	3	4	2

WORLD CITIES ANSWER (PAGE 23)

AFRICAN COUNTRIES ANSWERS (PAGE 42)

KNIGHT MAZE ANSWER (PAGE 31)

VACATION TIME ANSWERS (PAGE 35)

BRAIN TICKLER SUDOKU ANSWERS (PAGE 44)

1.

5	6	2	1	4	7	3	8	9
1	3	9	8	2	5	6	4	7
4	7	8	6	9	3	1	5	2
2	4	6	7	8	9	5	1	3
9	8	1	5	3	2	7	6	4
3	5	7	4	1	6	9	2	8
6	2	5	3	7	4	8	9	1
8	9	3	2	6	1	4	7	5
7	1	4	9	5	8	2	3	6

2.

8	7	6	5	3	4	2	1	9
3	9	2	8	6	1	5	4	7
1	5	4	7	9	2	8	3	6
7	6	1	4	8	9	3	2	5
5	2	3	1	7	6	9	8	4
9	4	8	3	2	5	6	7	1
6	1	5	2	4	8	7	9	3
4	8	7	9	5	3	1	6	2
2	3	9	6	1	7	4	5	8

3.

9	3	8	1	2	5	6	4	7
6	1	5	7	4	9	2	3	8
2	7	4	3	8	6	1	9	5
8	6	2	4	1	3	5	7	9
3	5	9	2	6	7	4	8	1
7	4	1	5	9	8	3	2	6
4	2	6	9	7	1	8	5	3
1	9	3	8	5	2	7	6	4
5	8	7	6	3	4	9	1	2

4.

2	6	1	7	3	5	9	8	4
5	3	4	9	8	6	7	2	1
7	8	9	1	2	4	3	6	5
1	2	3	4	9	8	6	5	7
8	7	5	6	1	3	2	4	9
9	4	6	5	7	2	8	1	3
3	9	2	8	5	1	4	7	6
6	5	7	2	4	9	1	3	8
4	1	8	3	6	7	5	9	2

5.

5	9	4	2	7	1	8	3	6
6	2	8	9	3	5	4	7	1
1	7	3	6	8	4	2	5	9
3	8	7	1	2	9	5	6	4
2	5	6	3	4	7	1	9	8
9	4	1	8	5	6	7	2	3
4	1	2	5	6	3	9	8	7
7	6	5	4	9	8	3	1	2
8	3	9	7	1	2	6	4	5

6.

5	4	7	1	6	2	9	3	8
2	3	8	5	9	4	6	7	1
9	6	1	8	7	3	2	4	5
1	8	4	6	3	5	7	2	9
7	5	6	4	2	9	1	8	3
3	9	2	7	8	1	5	6	4
8	2	5	9	4	7	3	1	6
4	7	9	3	1	6	8	5	2
6	1	3	2	5	8	4	9	7

7.

5	2	6	4	7	1	3	9	8
8	7	3	9	5	6	2	1	4
9	1	4	3	2	8	7	6	5
2	9	7	6	3	5	4	8	1
3	5	1	2	8	4	6	7	9
4	6	8	1	9	7	5	3	2
7	3	2	5	1	3	9	4	6
1	4	5	7	6	9	8	2	3
6	3	9	8	4	2	1	5	7

8.

9	6	1	3	2	8	4	5	7
8	5	4	7	9	6	3	2	1
3	7	2	5	4	1	6	8	9
1	4	8	9	7	3	5	6	2
6	9	5	8	1	2	7	3	4
7	2	3	4	6	5	9	1	8
2	8	7	6	3	9	1	4	5
5	3	9	1	8	4	2	7	6
4	1	6	2	5	7	8	9	3

ASIAN CITIES ANSWERS (PAGE 46)

JUST HANGIN' AROUND MAZE ANSWER (PAGE 49)

ARE WE THERE YET? ANSWERS (PAGE 47)

NAME THE LAND MASS ANSWERS (PAGE 52)

1. ALASKA, 2. NEW YORK, 3. ITALY, 4. AFRICA,
5. AUSTRALIA, 6. ENGLAND, 7. CHINA, 8. UNITED
STATES, 9. INDIA, 10. EUROPE, 11. CALIFORNIA,
12. HAWAII

PACK YOUR BAGS! ANSWERS (PAGE 48)

CIRCLE UP ANSWERS (PAGE 65)

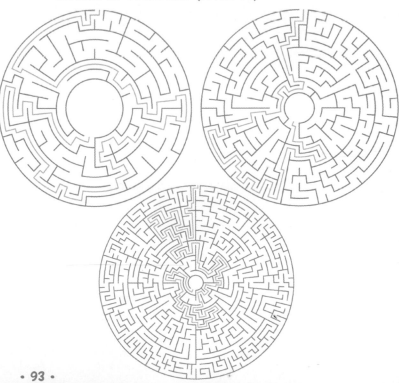

DOUBLE LETTERS ANSWERS (PAGE 70)

1. AARDVARK; 2. RIBBON; 3. SUCCESS; 4. ADDRESS;
5. FEET; 6. LIFTOFF; 7. JUGGLE; 8. HITCHHIKE;
9. SKIING; 10. TREKKED; 11. ALL; 12. MUMMY;
13. WINNER; 14. BAREFOOT; 15. APPLE; 16. CARROT;
17. PRESS; 18. KITTEN; 19. VACUUM; 20. REVVED;
21. BOW WOW; 22. PIZZA

WORD JUMBLES ANSWERS (PAGE 72)

1. MARK, ZOOEY, ROY: MOO YORK
2. FLORIDA, IDAHO, NEW YORK, NEBRASKA: FINLAND
3. BACKPACK, LUNCHBOX, ERASER, MARKERS: BAHAMAS
4. APPLE, ORANGE, GRAPES, CHERRY: RECHARGE
5. LION, BISON, GOLDFISH, ZEBRA: LOAF
6. BASEBALL, SKIING, FOOTBALL: ALASKA

NAME THE TOURIST ATTRACTIONS ANSWERS (PAGE 78)

1. STATUE OF LIBERTY, NEW YORK CITY; 2. TAJ MAHAL, AGRA, INDIA; 3. LEANING TOWER OF PISA, PISA, ITALY; 4. EIFFEL TOWER, PARIS, FRANCE; 5. COLOSSEUM, ROME, ITALY; 6. BIG BEN, LONDON, ENGLAND; 7. CHRIST THE REDEEMER, RIO DE JANEIRO, BRAZIL; 8. MOAI, EASTER ISLAND, CHILE; 9. ACROPOLIS, ATHENS, GREECE; 10. GREAT WALL OF CHINA, CHINA; 11. PYRAMIDS, GIZA, EGYPT; 12. PYRAMID OF THE SUN, CHICHEN ITZA, MEXICO

CHALLENGING SUDOKU ANSWERS (PAGE 80)

1.

5	9	7	6	4	1	3	2	8
2	6	3	9	8	7	5	4	1
4	1	8	5	3	2	6	9	7
9	5	1	4	2	6	7	8	3
8	7	2	1	9	3	4	6	5
3	4	6	7	5	8	9	1	2
1	2	4	3	6	5	8	7	9
7	3	9	8	1	4	2	5	6
6	8	5	2	7	9	1	3	4

2.

5	9	4	8	1	2	6	7	3
3	7	2	5	6	9	8	1	4
8	1	6	3	4	7	2	9	5
1	3	9	7	5	6	4	8	2
2	4	7	9	8	3	5	6	1
6	8	5	4	2	1	9	3	7
9	2	1	6	7	5	3	4	8
7	6	8	2	3	4	1	5	9
4	5	3	1	9	8	7	2	6

3.

2	8	4	5	9	1	6	7	3
1	7	5	3	6	8	2	4	9
3	6	9	4	7	2	8	5	1
5	1	3	8	2	4	9	6	7
7	4	6	1	5	9	3	8	2
8	9	2	7	3	6	4	1	5
4	3	1	2	8	7	5	9	6
6	2	8	9	1	5	7	3	4
9	5	7	6	4	3	1	2	8

4.

F	G	I	C	E	D	H	A	B
C	B	A	F	I	H	E	D	G
H	E	D	G	A	B	C	F	I
I	D	C	B	F	A	G	E	H
B	F	E	H	C	G	A	I	D
A	H	G	I	D	E	B	C	F
G	I	F	E	H	C	D	B	A
D	C	H	A	B	F	I	G	E
E	A	B	D	G	I	F	H	C

5.

C	H	A	I	D	B	E	G	F
G	E	B	F	C	H	D	I	A
D	F	I	E	G	A	B	C	H
H	G	F	A	E	C	I	B	D
I	B	C	D	H	F	A	E	G
E	A	D	B	I	G	H	F	C
F	I	G	H	B	D	C	A	E
A	D	E	C	F	I	G	H	B
B	C	H	G	A	E	F	D	I

6.

1	9	6	2	7	5	4	8	3
8	7	4	1	3	6	9	2	5
5	2	3	8	4	9	6	7	1
3	4	8	6	9	7	5	1	2
9	6	1	5	2	3	7	4	8
7	5	2	4	1	8	3	6	9
2	1	5	9	6	4	8	3	7
4	8	7	3	5	2	1	9	6
6	3	9	7	8	1	2	5	4

VANITY PLATES ANSWERS (PAGE 82)

1. JEALOUS PERSON: I M NVS (I AM ENVIOUS)
2. HOCKEY PLAYER: ISK8 (I SKATE)
3. SOMEONE WITH GOOD EYESIGHT: IC 2020 (I SEE 20/20)
4. IMPATIENT PERSON: H82W8 (HATE TO WAIT)
5. PERSON HAPPY WITH HIMSELF: GR82BME (GREAT TO BE ME)
6. OVERWHELMINGLY HAPPY PERSON: N XTC (IN ECSTASY)
7. ANOTHER REALLY HAPPY PERSON: U4 IC (EUPHORIC)
7. ELECTRICIAN: SHRTCRCT (SHORT CIRCUIT)
8. COMEDIAN WHO DOES VOICES: IMIT8 (IMITATE)
9. GARBAGE COLLECTOR: IMTCANS (I EMPTY CANS)
10. BASEBALL PITCHER: STRYK3 (STRIKE 3)
11. FARMER: 2M8O (TOMATO)
12. FLOWER SHOP OWNER: BO K (BOUQUET)
13. PSYCHIATRIST: HED DR (HEAD DOCTOR)
14. FOOD SERVER: W8R (WAITER)
15. POLICE OFFICER: N4CER (ENFORCER)
16. TEACHER: EDUC8R (EDUCATOR)

BACKWARD & FORWARD ANSWERS (PAGE 83)

1. DNA, AND; 2. PETS, STEP; 3. TEN, NET; 4. POT, TOP; 5. LOOP, POOL; 6. TUB, BUT; 7. MOOD, DOOM; 8. PAM, MAP; 9. FACED, DECAF; 10. GUM, MUG; 11. EVIL, LIVE; 12. WON, NOW

THINGS WE SAY IN THE CAR ANSWERS (PAGE 84)

OUT THE WINDOW ANSWERS (PAGE 85)

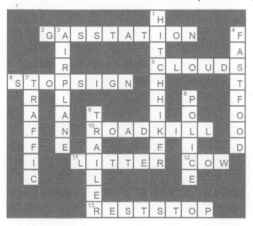

TRAVEL PHOBIAS ANSWERS (PAGE 86)

1. CLAUSTROPHOBIA (FEAR OF SMALL SPACES)
2. VEHOPHOBIA (FEAR OF DRIVING)
3. OSMOPHOBIA (FEAR OF ODORS)
4. ONEIROPHOBIA (FEAR OF DREAMS)
5. ACROPHOBIA (FEAR OF FLYING)
6. PEDOPHOBIA (FEAR OF BABIES)
7. NOMOPHOBIA (FEAR OF BEING OUT OF MOBILE PHONE CONTACT)
8. MYSOPHOBIA (FEAR OF GERMS)
9. HALITOPHOBIA (FEAR OF BAD BREATH)
10. AQUAPHOBIA (FEAR OF WATER)
11. ICHTHYOPHOBIA (FEAR OF FISH)
12. ANTHROPOPHOBIA (FEAR OF PEOPLE)
13. SIDERODROMOPHOBIA (FEAR OF TRAINS OR RAILROADS)
14. GEPHYROPHOBIA (FEAR OF BRIDGES)
15. TRISKAIDEKAPHOBIA (FEAR OF NUMBER 13)
16. NOSTOPHOBIA (FEAR OF RETURNING HOME)

COMPOUND WORDS ANSWERS (PAGE 88)

1. SWEET; 2. NECK; 3. SOME; 4. FACE; 5. WATER; 6. SUN; 7. BACK; 8. KEY; 9. SNOW; 10. HEAD; 11. HAND; 12. FIRE; 13. SOAP; 14. PIG; 15. CAT; 16. BLUE

EUROPEAN CITIES ANSWERS (PAGE 90)

USE THIS BLANK PAGE TO DOODLE,
PLAY A GAME, OR MAKE A LIST OF FAVORITE
MEMORIES FROM YOUR VACATION.